~~Jom~~

~~Jon~~

~~Vipmiyo~~

This book is dedicated to every child of color who thought they were not important enough to be represented in a book.

—T.

Copyright © 2017 by Travis A. Thompson
All rights reserved. This book or any portion thereof
may not be reproduced or used in any manner whatsoever
without the express written permission of the publisher
except for the use of brief quotations in a book review.
For permissions contact:
Travis A. Thompson
travis@thesivartgallery.com

First Printing, 2017
ISBN 978-0-692-94926-9
The SivART Gallery, LLC
www.thesivartgallery.com
www.thecolorwheelkids.com

presents

the Color Wheel Kids

Written & Illustrated by
Travis A. Thompson

Hey Friend! I'm one of the Color Wheel Kids. Have you ever wondered about where colors come from and how they work together? We, my friends are here to help you jump into our world where every color is important.

My name is Romeo Red and these are my pals Yasmin and Breyona.

Flip the page to get started!

Did you know another name for color is "hue"? As the Red hue I represent one of the primary colors!

I'm known as a warm color because I remind you of warm things and being hot!

I color some of your favorite things like apples, stop signs and fire trucks!

Hello I'm Yasmin Yellow and like Romeo I am a primary Color too, as well as a warm color.

I'm the color of bananas, baby ducks, lemons and brightly colored flowers like sunflowers!

My name is Breyona Blue and I'm a primary color too but I'm not a warm color, I'm a cool color!

I remind you of cold things like ice and water. People sometimes think of winter when they see me but I'm also the color of blueberries, bluebirds and the sky!

Did you know that as primary colors we can mix ourselves together to make new colors?

That's right Breyona! When I mix myself with Romeo we make...

ORANGE!

Hi there my name is Omari Orange. I'm made when Red and Yellow are mixed together!

I'm known as a secondary color! Secondary means I'm created from two different primary colors!

I'm the color of the Sun, oranges, carrots and fire. That's why I'm a warm color!

When I mix myself with Breyona we make...

Green!

What's up, I'm Germaine Green! I remind many people of the Earths land and that's why I'm a cool color.

I'm the color of grass, four leaf clovers and frogs!

here's one more cool color
nd when I mix myself with
Breyona we create...

Violet!

Hiya I'm VeNay Violet my nickname is Purple!

I'm the color of grapes, plums and even a flower that's called a violet!

All six of us are important and we have more friends who help to make us even better. Meet Bryn and Wendell.

I'm Bryn Black. I'm used to create "shades" of colors. That means a darker version of the color! Just like this:

I'm Wendell White and I create "tints" of colors. Which is a light version of the color.

I'm the color of doves and clouds and she's the color of black bears and blackberries.

Together we are the color of penguins!

What's special about us is none of us are better than the other. That's because each of us has a special purpose even though we look different. We are all needed to color the world! So remember no matter your color you are special in your own way and you are needed to make this world...

Words We Learned Today

Hue - another name for color

Primary Colors: Red, Yellow & Blue

Secondary Colors: Orange, Green & Violet

Warm Colors:

Red, Orange & Yellow

Cool Colors:

Green, Blue & Violet

Shade- a color with black added to it.

Tint- a color with white added to it.

Travis A. Thompson was born and raised in Charlotte, North Carolina. He is an artist and educator and this is his 1st children's book. Instilling pride in oneself is a core value for Travis and he believes this is something all children should be taught as well. Travis hopes to continue this journey with the Color Wheel Kids in the next book which will be titled 'The Color Wheel Kids: The Island of Forgotten Colors'. Travis loves all aspects of the arts and has enjoyed creating these characters. He hopes you have enjoyed this introduction to the Color Wheel Kids and will join him next time on their 1st real adventure to the Island of Forgotten Colors!

CPSIA information can be obtained
at www.ICGtesting.com
Printed in the USA
BVHW020251020222
627778BV00008B/643